The Good-bye Game

by Diane Cocca-Spofford
illustrated by Maryann Cocca-Leffler

ISBN: 1-58260-002-3

Manufactured in China.

10 9 8 7 6 5 4 3 2 1

Infinity Plus One
Ridgewood, New Jersey

To Cameron
Love, Mom and
Auntie Maryann

Every morning when my mommy and daddy work,
I go to the children's center.

My mommy drops me off in the morning.

My daddy picks me up at the end of the day.

I have lots of fun at the center.
I like my teachers.

I like circle time.

And I like jumping in the tumble room!

But there is one thing that
makes me sad...
saying good-bye to Mommy.

KRISTIN CAM TORY OLIVIA

Mommy clips her picture to my cubby.

She reads me my favorite book.

She even gives me a lipstick kiss tattoo on my hand. But I still feel sad.

Then one day, Mommy showed me a special envelope. She told me to close my eyes, put my hand in the envelope, and pull out one card.

My card looked like this.

"This is the Good-bye Game," Mommy told me. "Give me five kisses and three hugs, and your heart will be happy all day!"

We kissed five times.
We hugged three times.

Mommy said good-bye, and guess what?
I wasn't sad at all!

We play the Good-bye Game every day.
Now you can play it, too!